THE BOOK OF

THE DEAD MAN

OTHER BOOKS BY

MARVIN BELL

———————————

A Marvin Bell Reader: Selected Poetry and Prose [1994]

Iris of Creation [1990]

New and Selected Poems [1987]

Drawn by Stones, by Earth, by Things that Have Been

in the Fire [1984]

Old Snow Just Melting: Essays and Interviews [1983]

Segues: A Correspondence in Poetry

(with William Stafford) [1983]

These Green-Going-to-Yellow [1981]

Stars Which See, Stars Which Do Not See [1977]

Residue of Song [1974]

The Escape into You [1971]

A Probable Volume of Dreams [1969]

Things We Dreamt We Died For [1966]

THE BOOK OF

THE DEAD MAN

———

MARVIN BELL

———

COPPER

CANYON

PRESS

———

PUBLICATION OF THIS BOOK IS SUPPORTED BY A GRANT
FROM THE NATIONAL ENDOWMENT FOR THE ARTS
AND A GRANT FROM THE LANNAN FOUNDATION.
ADDITIONAL SUPPORT TO COPPER CANYON PRESS HAS BEEN
PROVIDED BY THE ANDREW W. MELLON FOUNDATION,
THE LILA WALLACE-READER'S DIGEST FUND, AND
THE WASHINGTON STATE ARTS COMMISSION.
COPPER CANYON IS IN RESIDENCE WITH CENTRUM
AT FORT WORDEN STATE PARK.

Library of Congress Cataloging-in Publication Data
Bell, Marvin.
The book of the dead man / Marvin Bell.
p.   cm.
ISBN 1-55659-062-8   – ISBN 1-55659-063-6 (pbk.)
I. Title.
PS3552.E52B65   1994
811'.54 – dc20   93-43415

COPPER CANYON PRESS
Post Office Box 271, Port Townsend, Washington 98368

Grateful acknowledgment is made to the editors of books and periodicals in which the following pieces appeared previously:

———————————

The Colorado Review: #8 and #11.
Denver Quarterly: #12, #24, #28 and #32.
Electric Rexroth (Japan): #22.
The Georgia Review: #23.
The Gettysburg Review: #7.
Harvard Review: "Preface," #9, #20 and #30.
The Iowa Review: #6, #13 and #26.
Iris of Creation (Copper Canyon Press): #1.
A Marvin Bell Reader (Middlebury College Press/University Press of New England): #3, #14 and #23.
The Massachusetts Review: #1, #15, #16 and #17.
Money (Peregrine Smith): #22.
New England Review: #21, #25, #29 and #31.
The North American Review: #4 and #18.
Orion: #19.
Poetry: #27 and #33.
Quarry West: #14.
Rhetoric Review: #5.
Sifrut: #3.
Voices (Australia): "Preface" and #10.
What Will Suffice: Contemporary American Poets on the Art of Poetry (Peregrine Smith): "Preface" and #10.
Xanadu 2 (Tor Books): #2.

DOROTHY

CONTENTS

LIVE AS IF YOU WERE ALREADY DEAD.

———————————————

(Zen admonition)

PREFACE

Before the Dead Man, minus-1 was still an imaginary number.

The Dead Man will have nothing more to do with the conventional Ars Poetica, that blind manifesto allegiant to the past. Let the disenchanted loyalist reconsider the process. Among motives, occasions, codes, needs and knuckle-head accidents, the Dead Man accepts all and everything. He knows in his bones that writing is metabolic.

What are we to make of the Dead Man's reference to Keats? That poetry should come, as Keats wrote, "as naturally as the Leaves to a tree"? To this the Dead Man has added the dimension of the minus. He understands that fallibility and ignorance are the true stores, the bottomless reservoirs of creation. He is the fount *for* that spillover. As for the tedium of objects distorted from their long imprisonment in books, the Dead Man has learned that to be satiated is not to be satisfied.

So he furthers the love affair between the sentence and the line. Whereas formerly the line took a missionary position, under the rule of the Dead Man the sentence once more invigorates the line. The ongoing attempt by dictionary makers to define "poetry," as it has been called, is an object of derision to the Dead Man. The Dead Man knows that every technique is passé except when reencountered at its birth. The Dead Man moves as comfortably among nightingales as among house wrens.

"Perfected fallibility": that's the key, the solace, the right number (one of one, two of two, three of three, etc.). Hence, the fragment is more than the whole. The Dead Man is a material mystic. His hourglass is bottomless. No. 27 ("About the Dead Man and *The Book of the Dead Man*") reminds us that the Dead Man is "a postscript to closure," and "the resident tautologist in an oval universe that is robin's-egg-blue to future generations."

Has it not already been stated of the Dead Man in the poem

"About the Dead Man and His Poetry" that he is the tautologist, the postscript, perfected fallibility, etc.? Yes. The Dead Man tells the truth the first time. The Dead Man, too, writes as he has to—with a watch cap and a sweat shirt, with a leaking skull and dilapidated lungs, at an hour beyond clocks. He lives on hunger. He eats his words.

Before the birth of the Dead Man, it was not possible to return. It was not possible, it was pre-conceptual, it was discretionary to the point of chaos and accident to return, since of course there was nowhere yet to return to. Since the birth of the Dead Man, however, it is possible, even likely, that one may return. From the future, one walks ever more slowly into the past.

All this the Dead Man knows. As for me, I know nothing. But do not think one can know nothing so easily. It has taken me many years.

M. B.

THE BOOK OF

THE DEAD MAN

———————————————

THE BOOK OF THE DEAD MAN (#1)

1. About the Dead Man

The dead man thinks he is alive when he sees blood in his stool.
Seeing blood in his stool, the dead man thinks he is alive.
He thinks himself alive because he has no future.
Isn't that the way it always was, the way of life?
Now, as in life, he can call to people who will not answer.
Life looks like a white desert, a blaze of today in which nothing
     distinct can be made out, seen.
To the dead man, guilt and fear are indistinguishable.
The dead man cannot make out the spider at the center of its web.
He cannot see the eyelets in his shoes and so wears them unlaced.
He reads the large type and skips the fine print.
His vision surrounds a single tree, lost as he is in a forest.
From his porcelain living quarters, he looks out at a fiery plain.
His face is pressed against a frameless window.
Unable to look inside, unwilling to look outside, the man who is dead
     is like a useless gift in its box waiting.
It will have its yearly anniversary, but it would be wrong to call it a
     holiday.

2. More About the Dead Man

The dead man can balance a glass of water on his head without
     trembling.
He awaits the autopsy on the body discovered on the beach beneath
     the cliff.
Whatever passes through the dead man's mouth is expressed.
Everything that enters his mouth comes out of it.
He is willing to be diagnosed, as long as it won't disturb his future.
Stretched out, he snaps back like elastic.
Rolled over, he is still right-side-up.

When there is no good or bad, no useful or useless, no up, no down,
no right way, no perfection, then okay it's not necessary that
there be direction: up is down.
The dead man has the rest of his life to wait for color.
He finally has a bird's-eye view of the white hot sun.
He finally has a complete sentence, from his head to his feet.
He is, say, America, but he will soon be, say, Europe.
It will be necessary merely to cross the ocean and pop up in the new
land, and the dead man doesn't need to swim.
It's the next best thing to talking to people in person.

THE BOOK OF THE DEAD MAN (#2)

1. First Postscript: About the Dead Man

The dead man thinks he is alive when he hears his bones rattle.
Hearing his bones rattle, the dead man thinks he is alive.
He thinks himself alive because, what else would he think?
Now he can love and suffer, as in life, and live alone.
The dead man no longer hears the higher register of the chandelier.
The dead man listens for pedal notes and thunder, tubas and
      bassoons.
He reads lips without telling anyone, but others know.
He can no longer scratch his back so he stands near walls.
To the dead man, substance and meaning are one.
To the dead man, green and black are not estranged, nor blue and
      gray, nor here and there, nor now and then.
The dead man has separate sets of eyes for here and there.
In the dead man's world, all time and stories are abstract.
In a concrete house with real walls, he lies down with the news.
The screen's flickering pixels are to him eyelets through which the
      world each morning is laced up for the day.
The dead man rises from his bed at night with great effort.
He is a rolling map of veins, a hilly country built on flatland.
The map of the body is of no use to the dead man.
When the dead man turns his neck, it's something to see from
      a distance.

2. Second Postscript: More About the Dead Man

Asleep, the dead man sinks to the bottom like teeth in water.
Whatever came to be by love or entropy, all that sprouted and grew,
      all that rotted and dissolved, whatever he saw, heard, felt,
      tasted or smelled, every wave and breeze has its metabolic
      equivalent in his dreams.

He is the bones, teeth and pottery shards to be claimed eons hence.

He is the multifaceted flag of each deciduous tree, reenacting time.

The dead man will not go away, the dead man holds up everything
with his elegant abstentions.

All his life he had something to say and a string on his finger.

The dead man will be moving to Florida or Maine, or sailing to
California, or perhaps he is staying put.

He has only to say where he wishes to be, and it can be arranged.

Inside the dead man, there is still a mellow sparking of synapses.

Unsent messages pool on the wavery deck, hit tunes that would last
forever, jokes that never staled.

The dead man is an amphitheater of dramatic performances,
ethereal scripts now written in the air like used radio signals
in space.

The dead man mistakes natural disasters for applause – erosion in
Carolina, quakes in California.

The dead man's shoes are muddy from being constantly on stage.

THE BOOK OF THE DEAD MAN (#3)

1. ABOUT THE BEGINNINGS OF THE DEAD MAN

When the dead man throws up, he thinks he sees his inner life.
Seeing his vomit, he thinks he sees his inner life.
Now he can pick himself apart, weigh the ingredients, research
      his makeup.
He wants to study things outside himself if he can find them.
Moving, the dead man makes the sound of bone on bone.
He bends a knee that doesn't wish to bend, he raises an arm that
      argues with a shoulder, he turns his head by throwing it wildly
      to the side.
He envies the lobster the protective sleeves of its limbs.
He believes the jellyfish has it easy, floating, letting everything pass
      through it.
He would like to be a starfish, admired for its shape long after.
Everything the dead man said, he now takes back.
Not as a lively young man demonstrates sincerity or regret.
A young dead man and an old dead man are two different things.
A young dead man is oil, an old dead man is water.
A young dead man is bread and butter, an old dead man is bread and
      water – it's a difference in construction, also architecture.
The dead man was there in the beginning: to the dead man, the sky is
      a crucible.
In the dead man's lifetime, the planet has changed from lava to ash
      to cement.
But the dead man flops his feathers, he brings his wings up over his
      head and has them touch, he bends over with his beak to the
      floor, he folds and unfolds at the line where his armor creases.
The dead man is open to change and has deep pockets.
The dead man is the only one who will live forever.

2. More About the Beginnings of the Dead Man

One day the dead man looked up into the crucible and saw the sun.
The dead man in those days held the sky like a small globe, like a
      patchwork ball, like an ultramarine bowl.
The dead man softened it, kneaded it, turned it and gave it volume.
He thrust a hand deep into it and shaped it from the inside out.
He blew into it and pulled it and stretched it until it became full-
      sized, a work of art created by a dead man.
The excellence of it, the quality, its character, its fundamental
      nature, its *raison d'être*, its "it" were all indebted to the
      dead man.

The dead man is the flywheel of the spinning planet.
The dead man thinks he can keep things the same by not moving.
By not moving, the dead man maintains the status quo at the center
      of change.
The dead man, by not moving, is an explorer: he follows his nose.
When it's not personal, not profound, he can make a new world
      anytime.
The dead man is the future, was always the future, can never be
      the past.
Like God, the dead man existed before the beginning, a time marked
      by galactic static.
Now nothing remains of the first static that isn't music, fashioned
      into melody by the accidents of interval.
Now nothing more remains of silence that isn't sound.
The dead man has both feet in the past and his head in the clouds.

THE BOOK OF THE DEAD MAN (#4)

1. Shoes, Lamp and Wristwatch

The dead man has a fixation on shoes.
Seeing his shoes, he cannot take his eyes off them.
Shoes, lamp and wristwatch – these are the basics, the elements,
    the factors.
The dead man factors-in time, light and travel.
So much depends on going, seeing and knowing: shoes, lamp and
    wristwatch.
The dead man embodies light and time at a distance: shoes, lamp
    and wristwatch.
The dead man wears his heart on his sleeve, but it's not what you
    think.
On the dead man's stopped watch, the time is always right.
The dead man's lamp is a dead man's lamp – on or off.
The dead man's ill-fitting footwear is never uncomfortable.
Long since the dead man made a fetish of entropy – shoes, lamp
    and wristwatch.

2. More About the Dead Man's Shoes, Lamp and Wristwatch

The dead man's shoes are two columns of x's, two fabricated facts,
    two tricks propped up by the heels.
The dead man's lamp is a hole in the roof, a gossamer shaft, a porous
    umbrella.
The dead man's wristwatch is a plaque with straps, a black and white
    picture of local knowledge.
The dead man learns by looking up and down, he values stamina, he
    assumes that all stories are apocryphal.

Thus, the dead man's time is time and no time, his lamp is light and
no light, and his two shoes do not prevent his two feet from
touching the earth.
By fictive lamplight, on the days of the mythic calendar, the dead
man stands upright but weightless in his still beautiful shoes.

THE BOOK OF THE DEAD MAN (#5)

1. About the Dead Man and Pain

When the dead man's ankle breaks, he is stoical.
Being stoical, the dead man is not hobbled by a broken ankle.
The dead man doesn't fear pain; he simply has no use for it.
When he breaks an ankle, he uses the other one.
When he breaks both ankles, he uses his arms, etc.
The dead man is like quadriplegics who grip the paintbrush with
     their teeth, the paralyzed who sip and puff to get around in
     their chairs.
Language lingers in the dead man after the event.
In his pre-Socratic period, the dead man raced against Achilles.
You thought I was going to say he raced against time, but no, it was
     Achilles, Achilles-the-Warrior, Achilles-the-Fleet, Achilles-
     the-Unbeatable.
Zeno-the-Philosopher gave the signal to start, and the dead man
     inched forward.
Achilles thought about running but did not move, he considered
     starting but did not take a step, he wondered about his
     indecision but did not contract a muscle.
Thus it was that the dead man, slow of foot, defeated Achilles.
Hence it came to pass that Achilles fell to a dead man, one of the
     precursor events of the future in which the dead man would
     forever be victorious.

2. More About the Dead Man and Pain

The dead man's condition is chronic, no longer acute, a constant
     state of being.
Because the dead man is in a constant state of being, his condition is
     chronic, no longer acute.
He thinks that language will be the death of us so he prefers gestures.

Now he points by implication, directs by nuance, gathers and
distributes atoms of information, the vapor of data, the ether
of ions – all without changing his position.
Pain to the dead man mirrors his long refusal, his wordless challenge
to the burning ceiling he used to call "sky."
The dead man spits in the eye of pain, he dismisses it with a gesture.
When the dead man thinks about pain, he thinks about being alive,
that's how he knew he was.
When there is no pain, no welcoming, no hospitality, no disdain,
there's no need to be stoical, the opportunity itself becomes
disingenuous, emotion embodied in all things including gases.
When there is no pain, no fallacy is pathetic.
The dead man argues to lose, he articulates his ideas only to see them
blurred, he expresses himself knowing his works are being
written to be erased.
The dead man behaves stoically only because he thinks it to be the
final proof of life.
In his unfeeling comprehension of pain, the dead man behaves
as if it hurts.
The dead man is like a stone reduced to tears.

THE BOOK OF THE DEAD MAN (#6)

1. ABOUT THE DEAD MAN'S SPEECH

Will the dead man speak? Speak, says the lion, and the dead man
    makes the sound of a paw in the dirt.
When the dead man paws the dirt, lions feel the trembling of the
    pride.
Speak, says the tree, and the dead man makes the sound of tree bark
    enlarging its circumference, a slight inhalation.
Speak, says the wind, and the dead man exhales all at once.
Whoever told the dead man to be quiet was whistling in the dark.
To the dead man, the dark is all words as white is all colors.
The dead man obliges, he cooperates, he speaks when spoken to, so
    when the dirt says Speak, he says what erosion says.
And when the air says Speak, the dead man says what a cavity says.
The dead man knows the syntax of rivers and rocks, the one a long
    ever-qualifying sentence for which no last words suffice, the
    other the briefest and most steadfast exercise in exclusion.
The dead man is a rock carried by a river, a pebble borne by air, a
    sound carved into frequencies infrequently registered.

2. MORE ABOUT THE DEAD MAN'S SPEECH

The dead man is part of the chorus that sings the music of the
    spheres.
Dead man's music uses the harmonics and parasitics of sound, in
    bands of low frequencies caught in ground waves that hug the
    terrain as they go, and in ultrahigh megacycles that dent the
    ionosphere and refract over the horizon.
The dead man makes no distinction between the music he hears and
    the music he only knows about.
There are five elements in the dead man's music (time, tempo, key,
    harmony and counterpoint) and two factors (silence and
    chance).

To the dead man, the wrinkled back of a hand is a score to be read.
The balding top and back of his head are a kind of braille awaiting a
     blind conductor.
The dead man's bone-sounds and teeth-clacks are a form of tuning up.
Sad music brings artificial tears to the dead man's dilated eyes.
All things being equal, the dead man is not fussy about pitch and
     dissonance.
His inner ear is set to hear euphonic consonants.
The dead man sings in the shower, in good weather and bad, without
     knowing a song.
He hums the tunes of commercials without the words, sympathetic
     vibrations.
He has ideas for musical instruments made of roots and feathers,
     harps that use loose dirt something like an interrupted
     hourglass.
When the dead man, in a gravelly voice, sings gospel, hammers
     descend upon anvils.

THE BOOK OF THE DEAD MAN (#7)

1. About the Dead Man and the National Pastime

When the dead man sees a rock, he remembers the hidden ball trick.
Remembering the hidden ball trick, the dead man sees a rock.
Now he can pick it up and throw it to no one, the *acte gratuité*.
Now he can make them pay dearly for the long lead off first.
The hidden ball trick is subterfuge, but so what?, nothing the dead
      man does violates the spirit of the game.
The dead man practices the decoy, forcing runners to slide.
Running from third for home with one out, tie score, bottom of the
      ninth, he delays, then bowls over the catcher, letting the
      runner from second score between his legs.
He steals second, then steals first, second, first, until the catcher
      throws wildly into the outfield and a runner scores from third.
He throws a potato back to the pitcher after a pickoff play.
He drops his bat in the batting box and takes a miniature step
      backwards to cause a balk.
The dead man feels the spirit of the game in his bones.
He understands the long windup, the walk to the mound, the interval
      between hit and error, the stopped seams on a hanging curve.
The dead man knows why the players don't step on the chalk lines as
      they change from out to up and up to out.

2. More About the Dead Man and the National Pastime

The dead man remembers the great individualists: Ruth swinging
      just beneath his pot belly, DiMaggio's spread stance,
      Williams' super-vision, Reiser hitting the outfield walls to
      catch flies before padding, Newsom sitting down after whiffing
      and then trying to run for it from the dugout, Musial coiled at
      bat like a question mark, Satchel Paige above all who said not
      to look back, Lopat's junk, Veeck's midget, the spit and
      Vaseline specialists, the cutters.

The dead man can go on and on if it goes into extra innings.

To the dead man, a good arm means more than a good stick.

The dead man likes scoreless games with plenty of runners.

The dead man stands in the on deck circle admiring the trademark
of his bat.

He sights along the handle, he taps it to listen for cracks, he rubs
pine tar up and down oozing with anticipation.

The inning ends before the dead man can bat.

If it takes a great play, a double play, a triple play, no matter what,
the dead man beats the curfew.

The dead man died from pennant fever but was resurrected by a
Texas League pop-up which landed nearby and which he is
keeping hidden until the end of the seventh inning stretch.

THE BOOK OF THE DEAD MAN (#8)

1. About the Dead Man's Head

The dead man puts another head on his shoulder and thinks he's a
     Siamese twin.
He thinks he's a Siamese twin when he puts another head on his
     shoulder.
"Double or nothing" is the dead man's motto.
He has other mottoes: "A stitch in time sews heaven to earth" and
     "No pain, no end to pain."
The dead man thinks he's a Siamese twin because one head cannot
     hold everything he is feeling.
The dead man has migraines from too much data, pinpricks of
     discrete events in the metaphysical.
Random neural firings in the dead man produce predictive dreams
     among an infinite number of occasions, occurrences, chances,
     so why not double it.
Musketry and bee sounds in the dead man's ears are penny ante
     compared to the wealth of petrified knowledge he already
     contains.

2. More About the Dead Man's Head

When the dead man stays up too late, his brain empties out, *whoosh*.
When the dead man's brain makes that sound, *whoosh*, it empties
     out.
The dead man knows it's late but not how late, he likes the people
     who come to see him but doesn't know who they are, he is old
     and senses that he needs a fresh brain.
The dead man holds up a skull and addresses himself, like Hamlet,
     but the words "to be or not to be" ring hollow.
No tragedy can occur unless the dead man can fall from a high place.

It will take years to stage the event: a calving glacier, a bursting
        volcano, a sudden fissure into which fall the flaws of temporal
        foundations.
A former tragedian, the dead man undergoes a change of heart.
The dead man's laughter increases in the abscesses and hollows, his
        body is a corridor of comedy, his cavernous hilarity wreaks
        havoc among the divisive.
When the comic and tragic split, the dead man feels like
        Siamese twins.
The presence of the dead man means two of everything.

THE BOOK OF THE DEAD MAN (#9)

1. About the Dead Man and Nature

When the dead man emerges in high grass, he thinks he sees his
shadow.
Thinking he sees his shadow, the dead man emerges in waist-high
grass.
The dead man has sewn dunes in Indiana, set pine groves in New
Jersey, combed tidal flats in Washington, chipped the rocky
flanks of Oregon and Maine, twisted seaweed in the Pacific,
constellated Atlantic beaches in fossil teeth: the dead man
knows the land first hand.
The dead man has been swept by date palms, fig trees, weeping
willows, live oak, he has felt beach grass and kudzu, he has
crossed lava and baked sand: the dead man's understanding
blankets the planet.
The dead man has seen the green wink of the declining sun.
To the dead man, fog is a mirror, a buttress against the distance.
The dead man's face appears to him among the clouds.
The dead man knows what he looks like in all things because, who
would better?
To the question, Why is the dead man the conscience of the planet,
the dead man's refusal to reply constitutes a final why not?
The dead man's didactics have an air of criminal vinegar.
The dead man, thought to be disintegrating, dissolving and
deconstructing, all the while has been materializing,
coalescing and under-structuring.
His is the composition of heavenly music, atomic constellations
echoing that subatomic groundwork for which he is
better known.
Without the dead man, the sunflower would not proclaim its common
face, nor the lily sway into biblical cover.

Freeze the dead man out and the natural world stops making love and babies.

But include the dead man, invite his willing reticence that bespeaks essence to the core, and the world oozes with spring and love songs to Proserpine.

Eurydice depends on the dead man too.

2. More About the Dead Man and Nature

Under his Malthusian covers, all is not lost.

Where survival of the fittest still reigns, the weak shall inherit.

Neither your friends nor the dead man's but someone's shall creep from the dank underside of wishes into the telling gift of then.

Nor shall the dead man be any the less for it.

For then shall the dead man come true, in every form of the invisible.

The hole shall be greater than any particle.

The present shall be greater than the future and the past greater than the present.

Such is the dead man's hindsight that can cap the lily with its own birth, unhook the atoms of a boulder, and turn the sea to seabed.

The dead man has experienced the future, what others see merely as the dark at the bottom of the stairs.

All is natural to the dead man.

"For that is what men do," says the dead man.

All men and women are in his thoughts today.

All are swept by the weeping willow where they lie hugging the dirt to stay low.

All but the dead man shall bow down before plenty.

All but the dead man shall bow down for nothing.

THE BOOK OF THE DEAD MAN (#10)

1. About the Dead Man and His Poetry

The dead man has poetry in his stomach, bowels and genitals.
In the dead man's inner organs, poems are born, mate, change
      and die.
The dead man's genitalia have caused him many problems.
When the dead man's writing is called "poetry," he laughs
      derisively.
The dead man sees no difference between a line and a sentence.
The dead man distributes definitions of poetry by reshaping the
      concept.
"Oh Dead Man, Dead Man," sings the nightingale of tradition.
"Dead Man, oh Dead Man," sing the masses of sparrows.
The dead man, like Keats, shall live among the English poets.
The dead man is perfected fallibility, the dead man shines without
      reflecting, the dead man is one of one, two of two, three of
      three, etc.

2. More About the Dead Man and His Poetry

When the dead man writes a poem worth preserving, he immediately
      burns it.
The dead man burns everything he writes, but pieces survive.
The fragment is more than the whole.
It takes its place among the apocrypha.
The dead man's poems are studied as if he were Aristotle and their
      subject *catharsis*.
For every book, there is one poem that sells it: a love poem or a life
      poem.
The dead man writes a poem to woo them in.
The dead man doesn't need to do life-writing. Oh windswept plains!

In the dead man's lexicon, a simple word for a thing, such as "tree,"
goes everywhere: its roots into history and prehistory, its
branches into entropy and time, its leaves into beauty
and belief.
The dead man looks into a cup of coffee and sees the plains of Africa,
and of course his face appears too.
When he looks down, there appear to him, in the panel of such
substance as his vision encloses, the matter and the matter-
with, events and their nature, the beginnings of inertia and
the end of momentum.
The entire world starts from the dead man's fingertips and from the
front edges of his toes, and in all things possible there is a
foreground right in front of his eyes.
The dead man refutes those who say they have nothing to say, no
subject, no data, no right, no voice except they first dip their
feet in the Ganges or tramp the Yukon.
The dead man sees the world in a grain of sand and feels it pass
through his hands.
He is the unblinking mystic of fiber, fluid and gas.
No manifestation bypasses his bottomless hourglass.

THE BOOK OF THE DEAD MAN (#11)

1. About the Dead Man and Medusa

When the dead man splays his arms and legs, he is a kind of Medusa.

Thinking himself Medusa, the dead man further splays his arms
and legs.

Now he can shake it, toss it, now he can weave a seductive glamour
into the source of all feelings, a glamour known to roots and to
certain eyeless vermin of interiors.

The dead man knows the power of hair by its absence, hairy as he
was at the near edge of immortality while his fame kept
growing.

The dead man uses the ingredients of cosmetic products made
just for men.

He pares his nails in the background, just as Joyce, the elder
statesman of rainy statelessness, pictured the alienated artist
after work.

He snips the little hairs from his nose and from inside the shells of his
ears, for the artist must be laid bare in a light easily diverted.

He wears the guarded fashions of loose clothing so that changes that
might offend – the loss of a limb or a sudden hollow in the
chest – may go undetected.

Mortal among immortals, the dead man can change you to stone.

2. More About the Dead Man and Medusa

The dead man mistakes his rounded shoulders for wings.

His shoulder blades suggesting wings, the dead man steals a
peripheral glance and shrugs, causing a breeze.

While the dead man's nails keep growing, the dead man has claws.

Once the dead man has lain in the earth long enough, he will have
snakes for hair.

Who could have guessed that the dead man was this much of a
woman?

Who knows better the extraneous ripple of a long yawn?

In the theory of the dead man, nothing accounts for his maternity.

The dead man will not move out of harm's way, nor leave his
children, he repeatedly gives his life for them.

Who else may someday be beheaded by a sword made out of water
and weed?

Mortal among immortals, the dead man strangles the moon in saliva.

Domed and tentacled, capped and limbed, the dead man resembles
a jellyfish.

Under his wig, the dead man's waxed skull belies the soft spot on a
baby's head that turns whosoever knows of it to mush.

The dead man speaks also for those who were turned into stone.

THE BOOK OF THE DEAD MAN (#12)

1. About the Dead Man and Mirrors

The dead man is a receptacle for ideas, not images!
The dead man forgoes the illusory world of action for the natural
        state of existence.
Hell, the dead man spits on the grotesqueries of artistic effort!
Orpheus, a notorious polyglot, couldn't go anywhere without looking
        over his shoulder.
The dead man sings songs denied to Orpheus without looking back.
The dead man holds a mirror up to nature in which none of it can be
        seen by whoever stands before it to look – well, of course!
This is the difference between the dead man and Orpheus.
The dead man wills his mirrors, his stickum stars, his window glass,
        his brass kettle, his crystal wristwatch, his flashlight – all of it
        to Orpheus whose days are dedicated to looking for himself.
The dead man is reflective, but you cannot find yourself in his eyes.
The dead man offers neither praise nor blame but permission to
        follow.
The dead man, outwardly calm, seethes with a wild enthusiasm.
The dead man's mirror shows the bones but omits the flesh.
The dead man has no use for the kind of mirror in which the moon
        can cut his hand.
He presses a coin to the face of a mirror to see how deep the image
        goes because he admires optical artifice.

2. More About the Dead Man and Mirrors

To the dead man, the surface of a lake is a window, not a mirror.
The dead man sees to the floor of the river where he watches carp
        and other bottom feeders eat the darkness.
He cannot swim but sinks to the ocean floor and crawls while holding
        his breath.

When the dead man hovers over a cup of coffee, he sees the grounds
and reads in their suspension a prediction of atomization.
In the eyes of another, the dead man sees a pathway to blameless
dreams.
The dead man misses himself, it is true, but only in the abstract.
Hence, the dead man shows no mercy to mirrors, his visage suddenly
appearing on the surface to those who run screaming from it.
To those who hated their parents, the dead man takes on the facial
attributes of a father or mother and slyly infiltrates the space
between the glass and its backing.
The dead man makes no distinction between smiles and wrinkles.
To the dead man, a mirror is a source, a reservoir of light waves
extracted from a world of appearances in which a backward
look may cause years of handsomely bad luck.
To the dead man, the world is prismatic: hence, the refraction of
each element in the model, each number in the equation, each
image, each statement, each crystalline midnight.

THE BOOK OF THE DEAD MAN (#13)

1. ABOUT THE DEAD MAN AND THUNDER

When the dead man hears thunder, he thinks someone is speaking.

Hearing the thunder, the dead man thinks he is being addressed.

He thinks he is being addressed because the sound contains heat and
humidity – or groaning and salivation.

Isn't that always the way with passionate language – heat and
humidity?

The dead man passes burning bushes and parting seas without inner
trembling, nor does he smear his door with blood.

The dead man can only be rattled physically, never emotionally.

The dead man's neuroses cancel each other out like a floor of snakes.

He is the Zen of open doors, he exists in the zone of the selfless, he
has visions and an ear for unusual music.

Now he can hear the swirling of blood beneath his heartbeat.

Now he can fall in love with leaves – with the looping lift and fall
of love.

Naturally, the dead man is receptive, has his antennas out, perches
on the edge of sensitivity to receive the most wanton prayer
and the least orderly of wishes.

To the dead man, scared prayer isn't worth a damn.

The dead man erases the word for God to better understand divinity.

When nothing interferes, nothing interrupts, nothing sustains or
concludes, then there's no need to separate doing from not-
doing or to distribute the frequencies of the thunder into
cause and effect.

The dead man speaks God's language.

2. More About the Dead Man and Thunder

The dead man counts the seconds between lightning and thunder to
      see how far he is from God.
The dead man counts God among his confidants: they whisper.
The dead man hears the screams of roots being nibbled by rodents.
He notes the yelps of pebbles forced to maneuver and of boulders
      pinned into submission.
He feels the frustration of bodily organs forced to be quiet.
He thinks it's no wonder the sky cries and growls when it can.
The dead man's words can be just consonants, they can be only
      vowels, they can pile up behind his teeth like sagebrush on a
      fence or float like paper ashes to the top of fathomless
      corridors, they can echo like wind inside a skull or flee
      captivity like balloons that have met a nail.
The dead man serves an indeterminate sentence in an elastic cell.
He hears a voice in the thunder and sees a face in the lightning, and
      there's a smell of solder at the junction of earth and sky.

THE BOOK OF THE DEAD MAN (#14)

1. About the Dead Man and Government

Under Communism, the dead man's poems were passed around
hand-to-hand.
The dead man's poems were dog-eared, positively, under
Communism.
The dead man remembers Stalin finally strangling on verbs.
And the dead man's poems were mildewed from being hidden in
basements under Fascism.
Embedded in the dead man is a picture of Mussolini hanging
from a noun.
The dead man didn't know what to say first, after the oppression
was lifted.
The green cast of mildew gave way to the brown stain of coffee
upon coffee.
Suddenly, a pen was a pen and an alligator only an alligator.
A pig in boots was no longer a human being, a dead man was no
longer alive though everyone knew better.
Now the dead man feels the steamy weight of the world.
He trembles at the press of the witch hunters, their clothes like night.
He has in his memory all tortures, genocides, trials and lockups.
He sees the lovers of pressed flowers brought down by botanical
poverty.
He sees the moviegoers, who kissed through the credits, stunned by
the sudden light after the ending.
In the lobby, the dead man's manuscripts went under coats and into
pockets.
Then they all went off to spill coffee and argue ethics.
The dead man is the anarchist whose eyes look up through the
bottom of the glass raised in toast.
The dead man is sweeter than life. Sweeter than life is the life of the
dead man.

2. More About the Dead Man and Government

The dead man votes once for Abraham Lincoln, but that's it.

That's all he's time for (one man/one vote), so the dead man votes for
Abe Lincoln.

The dead man votes with his feet, lashing his possessions to his back
as if he were Ulysses tied to the mast to resist the siren call to
stay put.

The dead man votes with a gun, disassembling it, beating the parts
into scrap metal for farm implements.

The dead man votes with wet hands, a fishy smell lemon juice
can't cut.

He comes in off the boat, off the farm, from the cash register and
the time clock to throw down a ballot.

The dead man is there when the revolution stalls in a pile of young
corpses.

It is the dead man's doing when the final tally is zero to zero.

The dead man is the freight man on the swing shift at the end of
the line.

The dead man remembers the railroads run down by automobiles,
the fields commandeered for storm sewers, the neighborhoods
knifed by highways.

The dead man thinks a dead Lincoln is still better than the other
candidates.

He knows that death stops nothing, and he hopes to be placed among
the censored.

His immortality depends on the quality of his enemies.

He sees a wormy democracy spilling from the graveyards, its fists
flailing at the target.

There is hope, there is still hope, there is always hope.

The dead man and his fellow dead are the buried treasure which will
ransom the future.

You have only to believe in the past.

THE BOOK OF THE DEAD MAN (#15)

1. About the Dead Man and Rigor Mortis

The dead man thinks his resolve has stiffened when the ground dries.

Feeling the upward flow of moisture, the dead man thinks his resolve
has stiffened.

The dead man's will, will be done.

The dead man's backbone stretches from rung to rung, from here to
tomorrow, from a fabricated twinge to virtual agony.

The dead man's disks along his spine are like stepping stones across a
lake, the doctor told him "jelly doughnuts" when they
ruptured, this is better.

The dead man's hernial groin is like a canvas bridge across a chasm,
the doctor said "balloon" when they operated, this is better.

The dead man's toes are like sanded free forms and his heels are as
smooth as the backs of new shoes, the doctor said "corns"
when they ached, this is better.

The dead man's eyes are like tiny globes in water, continental
geographies in microcosm, all the canyons are visible, now
washed of random hairs that rooted, now free of the
strangulated optics of retinal sense, this is better.

All the dead man's organs, his skin, muscles, tendons, arteries,
veins, valves, networks, relays – the whole shebang hums like
a quickly deserted hardware store.

To the dead man, a head of cabbage is a forerunner of nutrients.

The dead man's garden foreshadows the day it is to be plowed under,
agriculture being one of the ancient Roman methods for
burying the Classics, the other was war.

No one can argue with the dead man, he brooks no interference
between the lightning and ground, his determination is
legendary.

2. More About the Dead Man and Rigor Mortis

You think it's funny, the dead man being stiff?
You think it's an anatomically correct sexual joke?
You think it's easy, being petrified?
You think it's just one of those things, being turned to stone?
Who do you think turns the dead man to stone anyway?
Who do you think got the idea first?
You think it's got a future, this being dead?
You think it's in the cards, you think the thunder spoke?
You think he thought he was dead, or thought he fancied he was
  dead, or imagined he could think himself dead, or really knew
  he was dead?
You think he knew he knew?
You think it was predetermined?
You think when he stepped out of character he was different?
What the hell, what do you think?
You think it's funny, the way the dead man is like lightning, going
  straight into the ground?
You think it's hilarious, comedy upstanding, crackers to make
  sense of?

THE BOOK OF THE DEAD MAN (#16)

1. The Dead Man's Debt to Harry Houdini

The dead man thinks himself invisible because of Harry Houdini.
Because of Harry Houdini, the dead man thinks himself invisible.
He thinks himself invisible because, who is to say he is not?
Because of Houdini, the dead man allowed himself to be placed in a
      box and the box nailed shut.
Because of Houdini, the dead man lay down after waving valiantly to
      the crowd.
Because of Houdini, because of Harry Houdini, the dead man holds
      his breath.
The dead man is like the apocryphal yogi, inhaling but once,
      exhaling at the door to eternity.
The dead man can whittle a bone into a key, he can braid rope from
      hair, he can pry open a crate with his still-increasing
      fingernails.
The dead man listens for a word agreed to by Mr. and Mrs. Houdini,
      never divulged, to be used to communicate from the beyond, a
      word that can slither upwards, a word as damp and airy as the
      center of a soap bubble.
The dead man mistakes grace for worth, escape for thought, the past
      for the future, the sunken underworld for a raised stage,
      nonetheless the dead man will out.
The dead man thinks Houdini is a real Einstein.

2. More About the Dead Man's Debt to Harry Houdini

The dead man challenges the living to escape from his cuffs.
He accepts any challenge, any imprisonment, any confinement or
      stricture, any illness, any condition, and each time he lingers
      in the vise or jaws or jacket or cell before he chooses to appear
      again, always the picture of unrestricted beauty.

The dead man hides tools under a paste the color of his skin, his
teeth are removable tools, he has seen the plans sketched
in the dirt.

The dead man, like Houdini, is a locksmith by trade, a prisoner by
vocation, an escapee by design.

The dead man has as many layers as an onion, as many tricks as
there are trades, as many seeds as a melon, as many weathers
as there are winds.

The dead man is dying to get out of tight situations using the
technique of atomization.

The dead man may agree to lie in a frozen nest, to cling to a seashell
rinsed of life, or to hang in the ether, but then the dreams
come and he goes flying.

Like Houdini, the dead man has no intentions, only circumstances.

The dead man thinks Houdini the Einstein of escape artists, what
with his youthful brilliance and his redefinition of the
universe into here and hidden.

The dead man's broken wings deny gravity.

THE BOOK OF THE DEAD MAN (#17)

1. About the Dead Man and Dreams

"Enough," says the dead man, grinding his teeth, checking his bite.

"Enough," the dead man says again, with his lips met loosely and his teeth apart so that the hum resonates, a choral trick.

The dead man's music-to-the-max, he has the diaphragm to sustain high notes, he has the embouchure to flutter and slur, he has the circular breathing to eliminate rests.

Hipsters, bohemians all gather fully themselves in mid-century past to hear the dead man blow.

There's jazz there, and the dead man spots the spilled coffee of poets rambunctious for Ionics, potters who pull from the inside out, painters of inverse volumes, sculptors freeing prisoners from stone, it's a time when plenty get it.

Getting it's the secret, ask the dead man, technique is epiphanic.

Upping the ante's the secret, ask the dead man, vision costs.

Swinging after midnight, grooving at 2, being hot or cool, knowing the body, indulging in a feisty surrender – ask the dead man, his secrets are out in the open.

The dead man disdains metabolic hooey.

The dead man is always in motion, like a pebble dropped into a lake, like a finger stuck into an eye, like a permanent wish.

The dead man sings and plays as well in sleep as awake, he positively trumpets down the walls of times past.

The dead man dreams of the intimate, animated toys of childhood, through which pass the pensive clouds of adolescence resembling things removed to a safe distance, and the icons of free logic: sad-eyed violins, ships navigating the equator inside bottles, messages written in lemon juice, screaming candles and such.

Whoever comes before the dead man for judgment, he shall be judged.

The dead man fingers the suspect, he has nothing to hide.

To the dead man, logic is the light inside the crystal, refracted,
      unavailable otherwise.
The dead man takes a hammer to a piece of coal to let out a diamond.
He squeezes an ornament at Christmas to reveal the blood that was
      inside.
He creases the water at flood-stage, he shoulders the blame, he
      interrupts, he insists, he bends light.

2. More About the Dead Man and Dreams

To the dead man, North Dakota is in the closet.
The dead man makes no distinction between a map and a place.
The dead man is glued to existence, he is wishful and watchful but he
      doesn't need to know.
Things appear altered in his dreams: milk in black light, footwear
      rearranged by cubists, friends who talk out of both sides of
      their mouths like Egyptian figures seen from two sides.
If he could only have been white hair forever!
If he could have suffered indeterminately, seaweed tossed to and fro
      in sight of shore.
If he could have been a bottom feeder without having had to die!
Achhh, the dead man has dreams within dreams, he has the claws to
      grip an altar, he rolls up the dirt, he plies the waves, he rides
      the wind, he crosses time lines without touching his watch,
      everything happens at the same time.
From the dead man's point of view, perspective is a function of time,
      not space, so to him a dream is a whistle to shatter the known
      frequencies.
The dead man drinks from a fractured goblet.

THE BOOK OF THE DEAD MAN (#18)

1. The Dead Man's Advice

"Well, I wouldn't be so hurry if I was you."
The dead man starts with a wake, halbeit (sic) in salmon time.
"You don't know tunnel's end, but hell."
The dead man catches hisself pigeon-talking, neck over the moment
      unstill.
Like a pigeon, the dead man's iridescence aflutter.
Dead man carried aloft messages War-to-End-All-Wars, now extinct.
"What's rush, what's linger, neither of none's the one, where it
      ends."
"Who," the dead man, "wants to know?"
The dead man rubs the leatherette of his Dante, considering Hell.
He riffles the sheets of his Shakespeare, the revenge parts.
"You let *catharsis* out, you've got nothing."
"Your dreams mature, there's no childhood, best be dumb."
The dead man's got hokey and corny and the dwarfs of ideas that
      gambol in dreamland, that carnival tent, that circus of
      perpetual motion.
"I decent ideas crash and burn, sometime, Sometime."
The dead man sees the leaves sweat before they lose their umbilicals.

2. More Dead Man's Advice

Between a rock and a hard place, between sleeping and waking,
      between Gurdjieff and Ouspensky, among cattle and chattel—
Oh, the dead man goes straight.
Happenstance the location, circumlocution the path, the dead man
      towers.
"Unrapidly, you mean to get there, do you not?"
Oh the dead man, consent for resolutions, student of the betterment,
      refinisher, repairer, partaker of samples with the whole
      in mind—

Oh, how straight the dead man gone.

"You got blame to give out none, rightchyar?"

"Who," dead man, "there goes?" what with bearing wonderment.

"Kierkegaard, let's try," who proclaims laughter to be prayer,
        "what with his name lilting, that's something right off."

Having the requisites, lacing the particulars, bearing the burdens,
        tempestuous among frights and nights –

Oh, how slappy the dead man chokes time, Heimlich to make it talk.

THE BOOK OF THE DEAD MAN (#19)

1. About the Dead Man and Winter

When the dead man's skin turns black and blue, he thinks
	it is winter.
In winter, the dead man gathers and insists, slipping his collective
	unconscious forward like a blue glacier.
When flowers turn under, he sees the stars blooming above, florid in
	their icy reaches.
When leaves desert the trees, he reads the calligraphy of the limbs.
The dead man endures material eternity with a shy smile.
The dead man in winter envelops, he encircles, he reaches around
	him like the possibility of wings on a butterfly.
In winter, the dead man tries on chaos in its fixed form.
His hollow deformity lasts and lasts, his shapely presence maintains
	the look it was given: that much longer is he gripped.
The dead man knows why the cherry tree waits for spring.
The dead man senses the earth going to sleep, he feels the vast
	organism within which he is a brainy parasite sputter
	and collapse.
The dead man waits with the bear in its cave and the rabbit in its
	hutch in the snow.
To reduce pain and swelling, the dead man takes six months of
	winter.
The dead man swallows winter, he applies it, he rubs it in, he wears it
	for support.
The dead man's head in winter lies like a cabbage in repose.
Under a blanket of dormant weeds, he basks in the brittle formality
	of the gray salon.
When there is no adversity, no rise and fall, no ascension, no
	decline, no frost too early, no season too soon, then there's no
	planet too unstable, no ship in the sky better than another for
	the journey of a lifetime.

The dead man's white flame is the last trace of ash.

The dead man through the scrawny stalks of beheaded weeds offers up the slightest scent of a place where live fish wait to be thawed and roots fall silent.

No one knows better than the dead man the chalk made from common materials that accretes around each organism deprived of water.

The dead man in winter is not just winter.

2. More About the Dead Man and Winter

The dead man in winter is the source of spring.

The dead man turns equally to all seasons with the cachet of a guest only momentarily served and all too soon departed.

What do you mean, not wiping the glass of the dead man's fingerprints?

What do you mean, disengaging from his small talk to rush to the side of fake heads of state?

The dead man freezes out the relentlessly glamorous, he does not welcome the vain nor host the proud, he turns from photos with too much hair and tilted heads, he absconds before the heat goes on in the bedroom.

To the dead man, all social gatherings are wintry.

To the dead man, a turn of the head leads to an ear full of dirt.

Oh winter, the season of warm hors d'oeuvres and cold counsel.

The dead man is the drumbeat of winter.

Among the frozen, among the polar thinking caps and arctic questions, among the sled tracks and boot crevasses, among every poised paw print and running hoof mark, among the etched signatures of survival that everywhere mark the surface, the dead man models for eternity.

The dead man in winter is in heaven.

THE BOOK OF THE DEAD MAN (#20)

1. ABOUT THE DEAD MAN AND MEDICINAL PURPOSES

The dead man's press makes a balm of beeswax.
He squeezes nectar from the orchid long folded into a book.
Where the dead man has found the strength to fix his grip tighter is a
      sensuous mystery.
The dead weight of the dead man, you wouldn't think it, nonetheless
      hovers.
The dead man transcends gravity, clinging to the bottom of the
      earth, then to the top, first one side then another, impervious
      to the siren call of those frigid planets which patrol the
      heavens seeking the victims of black holes.
The dead man's astronomy is to be taken with a spoonful of honey.
To the dead man, erosion is a form of CPR and an earthquake is the
      natural consequence of the Heimlich maneuver writ large.
Writ large is the dead man's dosage of tranquilizers and
      antidepressants.
The dead man's remedy is to hold still, thus becoming a
      counterweight to the hyperactivity of government and a
      counteragent to the passivity of charity.
The dead man fights infection with the same alacrity he once used to
      effect the peace.
When the dead man sank into the ground for good, a cease-fire
      prevailed and nonviolence filled the void.
The dead man uses death and dying for medicinal purposes.

2. MORE ABOUT THE DEAD MAN AND MEDICINAL PURPOSES

When the dead man's fever breaks, he thinks the earth sweats.
Seeing the earth sweat, the dead man thinks his fever has broken.
The dead man suffers daily food poisoning from spoiled fish buried
      to fertilize pines, rotted corn plowed under for lack of a price,

waste water weighed by the ton, and countless variations of
    carbon whose days are numbered seeping from landfills.
The dead man is in the path of sewage plumes, but a cemetery that
    large cannot be moved.
Thus, the dead man must digest every chemical element to see
    what works.
In pain, the dead man puts repetitive phrases to an endless melody,
    he tries gum and mints, he coats his stomach with pink oxides,
    but the tremolo continues until he feels he will burst.
Now the dead man dines on mustard, now ferns, he swallows fungi
    unselectively, he sponges up chlorophyll from cut grass.
When the dead man first turned his back and left, he felt green
    again.
When there is no attachment, no necessity, no need, no outcome, no
    consequence of importance, then naturally sick is well, and
    the end leads to a green beginning.
The dead man uses legitimate substances to break the law.
Like other living organisms, the cells and viruses that accumulate
    under free enterprise visit upon the dead man.
The dead man catches cancer repeatedly.
Thus, the dead man reproaches Darwin's "Survival of the Fittest."
The condition of the dead man has been upgraded.

THE BOOK OF THE DEAD MAN (#21)

1. About the Dead Man's Happiness

When the dead man hears the thunderous steps of an ant, he feels
  eager.
Sensing the reaching of a root, the dead man swells with metabolic
  anticipation.
The dead man loves the snoring of the sea and the absent-minded
  whistling of the wind.
He doesn't need much if it will rain now and then so that the weeds
  can flourish and a simple buttercup can get in position to
  sully a nose.
He likes listening to an ear of corn.
He loves the feeling of the wood when he drums his fingers.
He grows giddy at the thought of elk contesting and wolves
  patrolling.
The dead man does not choose sides between fact and fiction, night
  and day, beauty and truth, youth and age, or men and
  women.
The dead man can spend fifteen minutes opening and closing an
  umbrella, what a contraption!, its cone changes to a triangle
  and then a parabola, reordering geometry.
The dead man has turned his back on the planed edge of memory,
  each face from the past now bears the freshness of a cut
  orange.
The dead man's blood can be brought to a boil by a kiss, but also by
  dumb remarks about cows.
The dead man is an outsider by choice, unwilling to give up even so
  much as the graphite dunce cap of a wooden pencil and how
  it feels.
The dead man is one example, the rest to be filled in.
The dead man has it all, even the worms and the dogs.

2. More About the Dead Man's Happiness

The dead man wanted more until he had everything and wanted
      none of it.
At nerve's end, the dead man felt frayed and scattered: the profit-
      takers wanted their share, and the bloodletters, the parasites,
      the actual doctors, the patient embalmers, the donors, the
      grocers, the tailors, the candy makers, and himself, too,
      lunging.
One day the dead man decided to keep himself as he was –
      saw-toothed, tilted, uneven.
The dead man decided to stay short, lose his hair, wear glasses, get
      heartburn, be pained, and thrill to his ignorance.
To the dead man, more mystery means more.
More fog, more vapors, more darkness, more distance, more time,
      more absence – to the dead man, all is everything.
Put it down to the dead man's love of the watery rays of starlight.
Put it down to the dead man's lamentations.
One day something in the dead man rose from his body with a creak.
Under blank retinal covers he felt himself fill with happiness.
When he saw that he had displaced his weight in water, Archimedes
      cried, "Eureka!"
The dead man did the same with substance and shadow.

THE BOOK OF THE DEAD MAN (#22)

1. About the Dead Man and Money

Strange to say it, but the dead man needs sleep.

The dead man comes from a long line of people who had to make
a living.

Therefore the dead man invests in futures: he eats.

He has working papers, he sells short and lives long, he leverages and
hedges, he is himself a product of the gross national effort.

The dead man follows a money trail like an aneurism on the long trek
to the brain.

Who but the dead man foresaw the collapses of October, March,
September, April, December, February, November, January,
May, June, July and August?

The dead man's ledger is red for "ought"-this and "ought"-that,
but he counsels not, lest he become the box turtle that tried
to race.

His lips tremble with the good advice he withholds.

His knees quiver with the thought that he might someday move.

The thought of making a million sucks his brain dry.

Everything about the dead man's situation suggests no-load mutuals.

The weight of money makes the skin beneath his eyes sag.

The press of dollars gives him a thick pain in the chest.

His bones are edging away from the spidery fibers of hundred dollar
bills loosed from the pockets of burial jackets.

Inside the dead man's nose there lingers the odor of clean currency,
a minty smell of ink.

Between the dead man's ears is the noise of hands riffling a wad
of bills.

The dead man's eyes have a greenish tint, on his tongue there
remains the residue of a rich dessert, and his skin has the
texture of shredded excelsior.

Strange to say, the dead man is like a plate passed among the
faithful, and the dead man needs sleep.

2. More About the Dead Man and Money

The dead man made a living – an outpouring of roses at the end.
The dead man made a living – the swaying of poplars by the sea.
The dead man is not blinded by the flare of economic downturns, nor
      deafened by boom times.
The dead man sees through the whitewash on the floor of the
      slaughterhouse.
The dead man hears the blood run backwards when the boss stands.
He knows the red mist in the eyes of the cutters when the whistle
      blows.
The dead man made bread and moola, a wage and a bonus,
      greenbacks and lucre.
The dead man, like you, fell from the branch when the season
      had ended.
The dead man, like you, lay underfoot as the pickers passed.
Like you, the dead man went up a tree into the clouds and cut it.
Like you, the dead man was nearly yanked overboard by a net
      full of fish.
Like you, the dead man, buying and selling, was bought and sold.
The dead man pays cash, he rates each and every economic
      ingredient beginning with the baker and his dough.
The dead man is certified, bonded, obliged, indebted and exposed.
The dead man's insolvency is a rush of water from a hole in
      Hoover Dam.
His deposits are earth, air, fire, water and time, which he draws by
      the lungful.
The dead man is legal tender, solid as a rock, good as gold.
By his will, the dead man disgorges his riches and turns *caveat
      emptor* on its head.
The dead man keeps no accounts.

THE BOOK OF THE DEAD MAN (#23)

1. About the Dead Man and His Masks

When the dead man thinks himself exposed, he puts on a mask.

Thinking himself exposed, the dead man puts on a mask.

Before he needed a mask, he wore his medals on his chest and his
heart on his sleeve.

The dead man wears the mask of tomfoolery, the mask of
assimilation, the mask of erasure, the scarred mask, the teen
mask, the mask with the built-in *oh*, the laughing mask, the
crying mask, the secretive mask, the telltale mask, and of
course the death mask.

The dead man's masks are as multifarious as the wiles of a spider left
to work in the bushes.

To the dead man, a spider's web is also a mask, and he wears it.

The trail of a slug is a mask, and the vapors from underground fires
are a mask, and the dead light of sunset is a mask, and the
dead man wears each of them.

The dead man curtained off the world, now everything between them
is a mask.

He weaves masks of sand and smoke, of refracted light and empty
water.

The dead man takes what the world discards: hair and bones, urine
and blood, ashes and sewage.

The dead man, reconstituted, will not stay buried, reappearing in
disguises that fool no one yet cast doubt.

He comes to the party wearing the face of this one or that one,
scattering the shadows as he enters.

When there is no one face, no two faces, no fragility of disposition,
no anticipation, no revelation at midnight, then naturally
years pass without anyone guessing the identity of the
dead man.

It is no longer known if the dead man was at the funeral.

2. More About the Dead Man and His Masks

The dead man's mask prefigures all *ism*'s such as surrealism,
   patriotism, cronyism, futurism, Darwinism, barbarism,
   dadaism, Catholicism, Judaism, etc.
Many of the dead man's masks are museum pieces: final expressions
   from Death Row, those startled at the last second in Pompeii
   or Dresden or Hiroshima, faces surprised in the trenches, the
   terror of furnaces and lime, a look formed from suffocation or
   lengthy bleeding or embalming.
The dead man apologizes for leaving a sewing machine and an
   umbrella on the operating table.
The dead man catalogs war memorials, potter's fields, he takes stock
   of undiscovered suicides, pseudonyms and all instances of
   anonymity.
The dead man's masks are composed of incongruous materials
   accidentally combined and are as rare and wild as certain
   edible fungi that closely resemble poisonous mushrooms.
He doffs his hat to long hair, moustaches and beards, but does not
   give himself away.
He greets the grieving, the relieved, the startled, the victimized and
   the triumphant without letting on.
The dead man's hands are twice as expressive in gloves, his feet
   deprived of their arches gain momentum in shoes, and his
   mask shields him from those who wish to trade knowledge
   for truth.
The dead man's first mask was a hand over his mouth.

THE BOOK OF THE DEAD MAN (#24)

1. About the Dead Man's Not Sleeping

The dead man squirms under a cow-jumped-over-the-moon moon.

Under a moon like the one the cow jumped over, the dead man
squirms.

He squirms because he remains a child who can't sit still, who stays
up nights until his brain has been wiped clean and his eyes
are dry.

He starts over, the dead man does, as a child begins each day.

The dead man in the morning is fresh as a daisy, pure as the driven
snow, crisp as a new dollar bill, and he smells like a baby.

The dead man in the afternoon is as dull as dun dirt, he is passive,
digestive and ruminative.

The dead man in the evening rummages toward midnight.

After twelve, in the a.m., then the dead man's lucent eyes look
inward, focusing and amplifying the dark to a black hole in
a skull.

The dead man is absolutely animal.

Hence, the unmoving dead man stores up energy to such a high
voltage that it can freeze you to him.

Hence, the dead man when active tingles with escaping protons.

When there is no balance, no even or uneven, no regulation, no
permissible range, no parallax, no one sunrise, then naturally
the dead man from a little salt on his tongue may concoct a
new perspective.

The dead man sees himself hanging from the hook of the quarter
moon.

He watches himself touch his toes around the circumference of the
whole moon.

Like the moon, the dead man's true face is in shadow.

Like the sun and moon, the dead man's visage is mistaken for a
forward facing attitude.

The dead man's positive portrait masks the necessary negative, the
flatbed of minuses that lead a charge to ground.

2. More About the Dead Man's Not Sleeping

The dead man's blood rises and falls with the days: Monday,
Tuesday, *Duende*, Wednesday, Thursday, Friday, *Duende*,
Saturday, *Duende*, Sunday, *Duende*. . . .
Within him mix the essences of all cultures: *duende*, soul, *joie de
vivre*. . . .
The dead man sorts through pure substances to concoct impurities.
To the dead man, all ingredients are at hand, every division and
subdivision of matter, each flavor, each scent of intention – all
at the bottom of the bowl, the outcome undeclared.
The dead man's bones are skeleton keys to history.
Only the dead man can unlock the past.
He is the neutral observer, the truce force, the peacekeeping
mission.
His nonviolence belies his years, his pacifism seems an edgy
avoidance when we look through our eyes instead of his.
The dead man will keep his word but he will not sanctify it.
In the moaning grass, the dead man hears a vernacular for all time.
The dead man's teleology is the busybody seesaw of an adult.
The dead man's Zen is the zero before numbers, a face of stone, the
child before the man.
Hurry to see the dead man shining with a hidden light.
Go quickly to witness the dead man deepening with time.
The dead man lives while others sleep.
He whirls in the darkness, a faint blur in a wide field of night, an
underground voice trying to soften the blows.
The dead man short-circuits infinity to bring life to the eyes of cattle.

THE BOOK OF THE DEAD MAN (#25)

1. About the Dead Man and Sin

The dead man's brain has undergone metaphysical surgery.

The dead man can only know what he knows, think what he thinks, and feel what he feels.

To the dead man, a sin is a small bird and many sins are many birds.

The dead man thinks vice is like dust or sand, something blown about.

The dead man's civilization looks the same in ruins, same things underneath the foundation, same things in the air around it, same indirection of swirling currents.

The dead man thinks rectitude a pile of small stones that keeps something in place.

To the dead man, rigor is the discipline of exchanging atom for atom.

It's the same story when the dead man meditates on anything at all.

A small bird is one of something that comes down in bunches.

A large bird is a universe, an entirety held from above.

Intentions keep things in place, and change is a material flip-flop, a swap.

The dead man believes the evidence at the ends of his fingers: a misstep.

The dead man takes his direction from the placement of his feet, convinced that a pair of anything is no accident.

The dead man feels the tractor turning up the dirt and the soil reassembling in the grave.

The dead man hears the anchor descend in judgment.

He feels the waves sneer at the boat it breaks apart.

He senses the confidence of the rain in going where it wants to, and the condescension of the sun as it recalls.

The dead man is privy to mistakes, the mixed flock, the broken shadow, the indefinite article of faith, the powerless totem, the broken altar, the stopped prayer wheel.

The dead man's fiercest teeth were reborn as dust.

The dead man mixes with those in black suits to hear who judges.

2. More About the Dead Man and Sin

When the dead man finds a coin, he wants it to be heads-up.
Before he picks up a penny, the dead man wants it to be heads-up.
The dead man's good luck is a weapon to vanquish dragons.
The dead man has seen dragons of such cosmetic skill that their scent
      alone flattered the willows into a fatal swoon.
He watches for the horrible bird feet, the feverish tongue, the
      armored complexion.
After many encampments, the lamps are tepid in the dead man's
      vigil.
The dead man has it in him to hold still, to abstain, to decline.
When there is no more luck, no far side to a hard edge, no final rain,
      no fatal dehydration, no unwelcome visitation, no lingering
      suspicion, no terminal judgment, then the dead man is all
      black cats and rabbit paws.
The dead man is marked by night-walking on the grass, by the
      crisscrossing of predator and prey and the celebrity
      pedestrian.
The screech of a bird is like a whining keel in the darkness.
The dead man feels the earth nod yes and no with the legacy of the
      righteous and the tide of battle.
The dead man does nothing with the proof at hand or the direction
      underfoot, neither does he long for an edge to his neutrality.
The dead man's good deeds are ever-bearing fruit.

THE BOOK OF THE DEAD MAN (#26)

1. About the Dead Man and His Cortege

Dead man says "cortege" because, who knows?, means to be watched
from a distance.
In dreams lost, the dead man unquestionably meant something.
Just as well the dead man's language not in the dictionary, good
outcome.
When there is no more approval, no okay, nothing sufficient or
appropriate, then it's just as well the dead man's words can't
be looked up.
The dead man inclines toward an erasable slate.
The dead man knows what Hobbes said and goes along from Hobbes'
perspective: "nasty, brutish and short."
The dead man holds to the horizon, the cause of perspective.
The dead man, not able to hold a pen to render, thus not having to
decide this side or that, doesn't see things Hobbes' way
unless he tries to.
The dead man thinks Hobbes was one of those grass-is-always-
greener fellows who went into the jungle.
The dead man is a preservationist, a nutrition conservative, an
inactive environmentalist rotting within the system.
The dead man's cortege follows him for philosophical reasons, the
students of supernal gravity.
The dead man makes no tracts, leaves no artifacts not in fragments.
The dead man's skin no good for bookbinding, too wrinkled.
The dead man's eyes no good for marbles, out-of-round.
The dead man's ears no sound-system, scattered parts for a
horseshoeing.
The dead man's bones skewer the architecture.
The dead man's veins and arteries no good for plumbing, stripped
threads and leaky.
The dead man's bladder won't hold air, so no balloon, no bellows.

The dead man's nails a poor mica, the dead man's hair bad straw.
The dead man's vocal chords no harp for a fork, won't hold a tuning.
The dead man's blood no good for oil, too much iron.
The dead man's shoulders a faulty yoke, ill-fit to the oxen.

2. More About the Dead Man and His Cortege

Drying, the dead man rises at dawn like active yeast.
At sundown, the dead man descends from that chemical pride for
      which body heat is the catalyst into the rag and wood vat.
The dead man is the chief ingredient in paper and in marks on
      paper.
Muddy blood is the ink in the leaves of grass.
The dead man's a craftsman of ivy, vines and the broken lattice.
The dead man testifies to wind, torn bushes and the clatter from the
      henhouse.
Placing the dead man is difficult, putting him away takes time, he
      knocks on the walls of a resonant cavity underfoot.
The dead man reappears by first light and last light, in olive light, in
      queer violet light, in blossoming light, defenseless light, torn
      light, frozen light, sweating light, and he himself is lit from
      within.
The dead man has the luminescence of rotting wood.
When there is nowhere to go to find him, no circumstance, no
      situation, no jewel in the crown, no gem of the ocean, no pearl
      of the Antilles, no map, no buried treasure, only woods and
      more woods, then suddenly he will appear to you with a
      cortege of wolves or foxes in the midst of your blues.
The dead man lives on Socratic dialogue and fungi.
The dead man has plenty of company.

THE BOOK OF THE DEAD MAN (#27)

1. About the Dead Man and *The Book of the Dead Man*

The dead man thinks he is hungry when he hears his stomach
    rumble.
Hearing his stomach rumble, the dead man thinks he is hungry.
He thinks himself hungry because he doesn't think he is no one.
The dead man repairs to his study to eat his words.
He lingers to watch the hourglass change from time to no-time.
He leans at the window to look for whitecaps, thunderclouds, the
    accruing ozone of a low, the yellow cast of tornado air.
The dead man's bones are freezing, though his skin is room
    temperature.
The dead man's nerves will not give up, his tongue refuses to quit, his
    brain saves up until it sparks, his blood abandons his
    extremities to go where needed, his pulse suddenly races, even
    his eyes lean out to feel before they see.
Now his hands fly about to put-his-finger-on.
Now he beats himself about the shoulders to fix his yoke in place.
Now he sinks into the soil, now he ploughs, now he rips away the
    artificial crops to roll about in the glowing fungi.
In his study, in his box, in his prison, in his socks, the dead man
    returns to the land from which he was raised.
The dead man bought the farm, his number was up, he was supposed
    to be done for, he had reached the end of the trail.
The dead man lives on hunger because, what is more filling?

2. More About the Dead Man and *The Book of the Dead Man*

The dead man thinks he is satisfied when he is satiated, a mistake.
He thinks himself fulfilled when he is no longer hungry, an error.

Now his eyeballs burn, his skull leaks, and his skin pales upwards
from his wrists.

Now the words – first words, last words – come to life on their own.

Here is "insect," the truly meek of the earth, inheriting the ink.

Here is "vinegar," the aftertaste of pleasure, soaking into the paper.

Here are "bones" and "love" getting together, and minerals ride on
the light from stars.

The dead man wears a watch cap to the lobes of his ears.

He yanks on his sleeves and unrolls the tattered bottom of his
sweat shirt.

His fever has broken that was induced, and the sweat dries with
thermal fury.

All that remains is *The Book of the Book of the Dead Man.*

Valéry, a terminal idealist, abandoned the ideal.

There is a moment when the dead man, too, cancels further revision
of the impure.

Thus, the dead man is a postscript to closure.

The dead man is also a form of circular reasoning, the resident
tautologist in an oval universe that is robin's-egg-blue to
future generations.

THE BOOK OF THE DEAD MAN (#28)

1. About the Dead Man and the Continuum

Music stirs the dead man to nostalgia, he bubbles, he ferments.

Under music, the dead man reflexively labors to bear the past.

His liver shrinks, expelling the speckled sludge of diners and
taverns.

His spleen sweats off a gray aura of languorous melancholia.

Dotted half notes and whole notes squeeze phlegmatically from the
dead man's windpipe.

The dead man's bones break new ground in solid geometry.

His blood vessels decant greenish oxides, a lifetime residue of
electrolytic conversion.

Every element disengages, every sinew unwinds, each organ tries to
start up to name a tune or recall a face.

The dead man can't say enough about particular purples, maybe
woolen, maybe hair dye, all twilights.

He won't come in out of the rain, he loves the outdoors because of
what happened there.

The dead man sleeps with his eyes open, so eager is he to catch
a glimpse.

He hopes to keep time in place by wearing a run-down watch.

He attempts to stop the iron filings from lining up after the magnet
has been moved.

He tries to trick the compass by turning quickly, he diverts the wind,
he downshifts to mock the continuum with herky-jerky
movements.

The dead man is the funster of metamathematics and metaphysics.

The dead man has perfected perpetual motion in the form of
constant gravity.

The dead man, in the company of all sentient beings, is on his way
home to the sun.

To the dead man, body heat is something to die for.

2. More About the Dead Man and the Continuum

Like Rip Van Winkle, the dead man is not dead, he is just sleeping.
When the dead man's eyes flutter, it is twenty years earlier.
He thinks the stuff that comes through the food tube won't be fully
    cooked for two decades.
He believes that the nuclear waste around him is beginning to glow.
He sees the toxins leaching through the canisters, and the purified
    water leaking from the survival barrels.
The dead man takes the future with a grain of salt.
He bundles himself in contaminated rootwork, donating what he can
    to the chlorophyll factories.
He flings himself on the timed-release capsules to keep the earth
    drug free.
Rip Van Winkle survived through indolence and woke in the future.
The Hudson was thicker than he remembered, and it carried him
    back.
When there is no clear water, no river for the first time, no river
    twice the same, no sure path to the sea, no cloudless mirror,
    then the stationary dead man is a world traveler.
The dead man, circling in a rowboat or lounging on the dock, could
    see ahead of him.
Time was, the dead man could see his face on the bottom.

THE BOOK OF THE DEAD MAN (#29)

1. About the Dead Man and Sex

The dead man lowers standards, ha ha, sinking, steadily sinking.
The dead man is jovial ha in the tide pool peaceful zzz among the
      tubers thoughtful uh uh in the basement ho ho creating
      humph humph the foundations of modern thought.
The dead man throws fuel on the fire.
The dead man throws in spoonerisms, being lone bonely, he gathers
      the wordless words, the articulation of knee jerks and other
      reflexive gestures, the spill of an orgasm.
He puts in the *whoosh*, the *ssss*, the *ahhh* and *oh oh oh*.
He is hot for the body, heaping moan on moan.
The dead man is the outcome of ecstasy, everyone knows it and
      wants more.
The dead man's lapidary but orgasmic, nothing new there.
The dead man is the depository of fixed form, the vault for a cool
      customer, safe harbor, still he loves the juiced up joining in
      the midst of love.
The dead man lets the clock expire to be there.
He is a sponge that never dries, absorbing the dark water.
Omigoodness, the dead man does things.

2. More About the Dead Man and Sex

The dead man speaks the lingo of sizzle, the grammar of quickened
      breathing, he states the obvious: more is more.
To the dead man, the new moon is a rounded promise of romance.
The dead man's wounded moon heals over each attempt to explore
      her and comes again to flirt in the dark.
The dead man's understanding of the moon goes well beyond
      her face.
It travels beyond her light side, reaching around blindly but
      with faith.

The dead man seeks the becalmed, the held, the immobilized in
    himself and sets it free.
Therefore the dead man studies the day sky to see the early moon.
He knows the moon is the better half of himself, that he is incomplete
    without her, and he cradles her on his brow as she rises.
All these things the dead man does and more.

THE BOOK OF THE DEAD MAN (#30)

1. About the Dead Man's Late Nights

When the dead man cannot go to sleep, he squeezes blood from a stone.

Remember, the dead man is lapidary but orgasmic.

The dead man extracts blood, bile, semen, saliva, hair and teeth.

He weighs fillings and counts moles.

He takes a look at himself in two mirrors at once.

Front to back, side to side, top to bottom, the dead man is a matrix of
       handprints, stitches, whiskers, tiny volcanoes where
       vaccinations took, mineral deposits left to unclaimed salvage,
       congealed oil of an insufficient tolerance, wax and water.

There are many ways to look at the dead man but only one way to
       understand him.

The dead man can pass through a keyhole, the lens of an eye, the eye
       of a needle, walls that have neither doors nor windows.

He can disappear and reappear, he can summon feelings, he can get
       down on his knees, he can wave from afar, he can tie himself
       in knots, he can twist a thought or turn it over, he can count
       sheep, but sometimes he cannot go to sleep.

What then does he say when it's why not?

He says absolutely nothing, precisely nothing, eloquently nothing.

The dead man has dissolved the knot in which his tongue was tied.

Whereas formerly the dead man was sometimes beside himself, now
       he is one.

Whereas formerly the dead man cohered in the usual way, now he
       thinks dissolution is good for the soul, a form of sacramental
       undoing viewed through a prism, a kind of philosophic
       nakedness descending a staircase.

He wants to be awake at the very end.

So the dead man gets up at night to walk on glass.

He tumbles out of his sheets to consort with worms.

He holds back the hands of the clock, he squeezes the light in his
       fists, he runs in place like a man on a treadmill who has asked
       a doctor to tell him what to do.

2. More About the Dead Man's Late Nights

The dead man mistakes numbness for sleep.

He mistakes frostbite for the tingle of anticipation, a chill for fresh air, fever for lust.

He thinks he could throw a stone to kingdom come, but he is wrong.

He is used to being taken for granite, for a forehead of stars or a swath of matted grass.

But the dead man is more than the rivulets chiseled into the marker.

He is far more than the peaceful view at the downhill border, the floral entry, the serenity.

The dead man is the transparent reed that made music from thin air.

His life has been a diehard joy beyond the sweep of starlight, he transcends the black hole, he has weight and specific gravity, he reflects, he is rained on.

The dead man does not live in a vacuum, he swallows air and its ill effects.

The dead man is rapt to stay the course, fervent for each spoke of the sun.

The dead man is mad to ride the wheel to the end of the circle.

THE BOOK OF THE DEAD MAN (#31)

1. About the Dead Man and the Dead Man's Beloved

The dead man and his wife have an ongoing conversation, make that
    discussion, let's say debate, call it a disputation, maybe it's an
    argument.
To wit: who gets to go first, the dead man or the dead man's beloved?
When the dead man's wife strikes the dead man's funny bone, a kind
    of electricity surges from his elbow to his pinky.
The dead man and his wife bump their skeletons together like keys
    in a pocket.
When the dead man strikes his funny bone, his arm goes rubbery
    and his pinky quivers like a ripe raspberry.
When the dead man and his wife bump their bones together, there's
    no disputation, there's thesis and antithesis, action and
    reaction, give and take, physics and geometry, but there's no
    discourse in any metaphysical sense.
Notwithstanding literary compasses and other mathematical,
    magnetic or gyroscopic conductors of sexual metaphor.
The dead man's funny voltage is all physical.
When the dead man comes, he goes, and when he rises, he falls.
The dead man is the only one who goes to the ends of the earth for
    his beloved.
To wit: if they can't go together they aren't going at all.

2. More About the Dead Man and the Dead Man's Beloved

The dead man asks the lanterns to please whisper.
He asks the horses to whinny softly and to paw the earth gently.
He requests of the shovel that it move slowly in effecting its sharp
    separations.
He beseeches the dirt to be soap, the flowers to be fans in the heat,
    the shadows to be blankets for the evening.

To the mourners, the dead man offers a shot of Frangelico in a cup of
    steamed milk, he calls it a "split fountain," remember its
    name.
The dead man suggests a line or two after the ceremonial text, he
    calls it an "aftergraph," it's beyond closure.
The dead man can light a match in the wind, he can open a bottle on
    a car door, he has ways.
The dead man can rub his stomach and pat his head, he can make his
    arms revolve in opposite directions, it's easy now to be
    akimbo.
What was so funny about the funny bone that the dead man
    cried out?
Who will win the argument in their sleep?
What was the word Houdini spoke from beyond, oh foil trumpets!
The dead man and his wife, being of one mind and frequently one
    body, warrant that their fondest wishes have been granted.
Agreed to, this day of days, in this month of months and year of
    years, by the undersigned, a.k.a. the dead man, the
    vouchsafer, the night custodian.
The dead man has bracelets in the skin on his wrists, rings engraved
    on his fingers, and the ache of love in his bones.
When the dead man lies down with his wife, he breaks into a smile
    because night tickles his fancy, strikes his funny bone and
    otherwise breaks him up.

THE BOOK OF THE DEAD MAN (#32)

1. About the Dead Man and the Apocalypse

When the dead man feels the heat, he thinks he's in the spotlight.
Engulfed by flame, the dead man thinks he's the center of attention.
The dead man rehearses the impending collision of Earth and
      the sun.
He hears the fly buzz and the snake retreat: sounds from the ebb and
      flow of global warming.
He feels the ivy wilt and the holly wither: victims of an intolerant
      greenhouse.
The dead man is perspective itself, the universal focused to a
      pinpoint, the microcosmic magnified to the power of
      uninsurable Acts of God.
The dead man is not the materialist but the material!
To the dead man, the melted paraffin of a candle is a slow moving
      bog.
To the dead man, the rose petals are a tornado and the eulogy
      high tide.
Natural forces are all the dead man has or needs, he deduces, he
      intuits.
The dead man at the beginning is likewise at the end, he finishes
      what he starts.
Now come the sequential nights of retraction, when the dead man
      recants.
Darkness supports the dead man's reversions as the porous days
      did not.
Now the dead man hears what it must have been like to have started
      the world.
He loiters in the holes of astrophysical theories, likely at any moment
      to break through with a hypothetical work stoppage.
The dead man alone understands what it means to do less.
The dead man more than others has what it takes to make something
      from nothing.

Above all, the dead man takes inventory from scratch.

When there is no measure of candlepower sufficient to enlighten, no temperature, no tolerance, no voltage, no current, no draw, no output, then it's historical lunacy to throw off a moon.

Yet the dead man casts bread upon the waters, he throws caution to the winds.

When the dead man reaches the Void, he may throw an empty eyeball into space to start the whole thing up again.

2. More About the Dead Man and the Apocalypse

To have come to an impassable barrier, to have reached an unbridgeable chasm, to have come to a stitch in the fabric, to a peeling veneer, to know that under the stone is a city of slugs —

Before the birth of the dead man, it was not possible to return.

It was not possible, it was pre-conceptual, it was discretionary to the point of chaos, since of course there was nowhere yet to return to.

Since the birth of the dead man, however, it is even likely that one may return from the future.

The dead man walks ever more slowly into the past.

The dead man still has the upstanding bones of all the erect, but he no longer knows how to walk.

The dead man sits to walk, lies down to walk, crawls to walk, walks by mistake, by the skin of his teeth, by the seat of his pants.

It is easier for the dead man to pass through the eye of a needle than to ride a camel to paradise.

The dead man is the living Diaspora.

Say about the dead man that he took nothing with him but left it all.

The dead man's love for you is timeless and free.

THE BOOK OF THE DEAD MAN (#33)

1. About the Dead Man and a Parallel Universe

Perhaps it is not so important that the dead man lives.

After all, the dead man deserts the future.

He squints to better define the distance, a darkroom procedure.

He drops his jaw to hear better, he makes a fist around each thing to
gain a better purchase, he breathes with his mouth open to
better catch the odors of food and inhales as he chews to
better free its taste.

He walks downhill whenever possible.

Thus the dust where the dead man lies is fluffy, as if there were a
shadow shape within it, a more perfect dead man.

Hence the face of the earth wears an expression of beneficent
indifference, confirming that too much has been made of life
and death.

The dead man will be tears freed of eyes, laughter and moans
independent of any contraption, a soul without devices, a
spirit sans tricks.

The dead man is Darwin's resolution, an ultimate promise.

After the dead man, how can there be a body of myth, he is the living
truth.

The dead man seems smaller only because of where one stands to see
him, this is mental parallax.

2. More About the Dead Man and a Parallel Universe

It is as if there were being woven a cloth shirt made of the fibers of
dead men, and of course it will be perfect.

People will take turns wearing it, each one imagining himself to be
its owner.

A true knowledge of it will banish weariness and ennui.

The feel of it will be like solace in the rain, its wearer will shiver once
and once only.

To the dead man, the universe is a negative of a negative.

Thus, the dead man's minuses combine to form the pluses of a
parallel universe.

When the dead man's effects have been fully distributed, his entropy
come to fruition, then the imaginary numbers combine to pile
up in reality, denial is replaced with permission, safelights
with daylight and the fourth dimension with a greater three.

The dead man is over the top.

Marvin Bell was born in New York City and grew up
on the south shore of eastern Long Island. At twenty-
two he left the East Coast, and since 1985 he has
divided his time between Iowa City, Iowa, and Port
Townsend, Washington. He has been the recipient of
the Lamont Award from the Academy of American
Poets, Guggenheim and National Endowment for the
Arts fellowships, Senior Fulbright appointments to
Yugoslavia and Australia, and other awards. Mr. Bell
is a long-time member of the faculty of the Writers'
Workshop at the University of Iowa, where he is Flan-
nery O'Connor Professor of Letters. He has been
called "a maverick" and "an insider who thinks like
an outsider," and is the author of many distinguished
books of poetry and essays.

''ANUBIS,''

THE COVER MONOTYPE,

IS BY GALEN GARWOOD.

THE PHOTOGRAPH OF MARVIN BELL

IS BY JAMES MORGAN.

THE TEXT TYPE IS BASED ON A FACE

DESIGNED IN THE EIGHTEENTH CENTURY

BY GIAMBATTISTA BODONI.

COMPOSITION OF THE BOOK IS BY

THE TYPEWORKS IN VANCOUVER, B.C.

THE DESIGN FOR *THE BOOK OF THE DEAD MAN*

WAS BEGUN IN PORT TOWNSEND, WASHINGTON,

BY TREE SWENSON

& CONCLUDED

IN CAMBRIDGE, MASSACHUSETTS.